GW00674724

45

LOVE
SONNETS

Selected by
Ian Hamilton

BLOOMSBURY
* POETRY *
CLASSICS

This selection by Ian Hamilton first published 1997
Copyright © 1997 by Bloomsbury Publishing Plc
Bloomsbury Publishing Plc, 38 Soho Square,
London W1V 5DF

A CIP catalogue record for this book
is available from the British Library

ISBN 0 7475 3731 3

10 9 8 7 6 5 4 3 2 1

Typeset in Great Britain by
Hewer Text Composition Services, Edinburgh
Printed in Great Britain by St Edmundsbury Press, Suffolk
Jacket design by Jeff Fisher

CONTENTS

THOMAS WYATT
The Hind

Whoso list to hunt, I know where is an hind,
But as for me, helas, I may no more.
The vain travail hath wearied me so sore,
I am of them that farthest come behind.
Yet may I by no means my wearied mind
Draw from the Deer, but as she fleeth afore
Fainting I follow. I leave off therefore,
Since in a net I seek to hold the wind.
Who list her hunt (I put him out of doubt)
As well as I may spend his time in vain.
And graven with diamonds in letters plain
There is written her fair neck round about:
'Noli me tangere, for Caesar's I am,
And wild for to hold, though I seem tame.'

THOMAS WYATT
Love Renounced

Farewell, Love, and all thy laws for ever:
Thy baited hooks shall tangle me no more.
Senec and Plato call me from thy lore,
To perfect wealth my wit for to endeavour.
In blind error when I did persever,
Thy sharp repulse, that pricketh aye so sore,
Hath taught me to set in trifles no store,
And scape forth, since liberty is liever.
Therefore farewell, go trouble younger hearts,
And in me claim no more authority:
With idle youth go use thy property,
And thereon spend thy many brittle darts.
For, hitherto tho' I've lost all my time,
Me lusteth no longer rotten boughs to climb.

THOMAS WYATT
No Peace

I find no peace, and all my war is done,
I fear, and hope. I burn, and freeze like ice.
I fly above the wind, yet can I not arise.
And naught I have, and all the world I season.
That loseth nor locketh holdeth me in prison,
And holdeth me not, yet can I scape nowise:
Nor letteth me live nor die at my devise,
And yet of death it giveth me occasion.
Without eyen I see, and without tongue I plain:
I desire to perish, and yet I ask health:
I love another, and thus I hate myself:
I feed me in sorrow, and laugh at all my pain.
Likewise displeaseth me both death and life,
And my delight is causer of this strife.

THOMAS WYATT
The Galley

My galley chargèd with forgetfulness
Through sharp seas in winter nights doth pass
Tween rock and rock, and eke mine enemy alas,
That is my lord, steereth with cruelness.
And every oar a thought in readiness,
As though that death were light in such a case,
An endless wind doth tear the sail apace
Of forced sighs and trusty fearfulness.
A rain of tears, a cloud of dark disdain,
Hath done the wearied cords great hinderaunce:
Wreathed with error and eke with ignoraunce
The stars be hid that led me to this pain.
Drowned is reason that should me comfort,
And I remain despairing of the port.

THOMAS WYATT
Change

Divers doth use (as I have heard and know),
When that to change their ladies do begin,
To moan and wail and never for to lynn,
Hoping thereby to pease their painful woe.
And some there be that when it chanceth so
That women change, and hate where love hath been,
They call them false and think with words to win
The hearts of them that otherwhere doth go.
But as for me, though that by chance indeed
Change hath outworn the favour that I had,
I will not wail, lament, nor yet be sad,
Nor call her false that falsely did me feed:
But let it pass, and think it is of kind
That often change doth please a woman's mind.

THOMAS WYATT
Scorn

My love took scorn my service to retain:
Wherein me thought she usèd cruelty,
Since with good will I lost my liberty
To follow her which causeth all my pain.
Might never care cause me for to refrain,
But only this, which is extremity,
Giving me naught, alas, nor to agree
That, as I was, her man I might remain.
But since that thus ye list to order me
That would have been your servant true and fast,
Displease thee not my doting days be past
And with my loss to live I must agree.
For, as there is a certain time to rage,
So is there time such madness to assuage.

HENRY HOWARD: EARL OF SURREY
Spring

The soote season, that bud and bloom forth brings,
With green hath clad the hill, and eke the vale.
The nightingale with feathers new she sings;
The turtle to her make hath told her tale.
Summer is come, for every spray now springs,
The hart hath hung his old head on the pale;
The buck in brake his winter coat he flings;
The fishes flete with new repairèd scale;
The adder all her slough away she slings;
The swift swallow pursueth the flies smale;
The busy bee her honey now she mings;
Winter is worn that was the flowers' bale.
And thus I see among these pleasant things
Each care decays, and yet my sorrow springs!

HENRY HOWARD: EARL OF SURREY
Vow to Love Faithfully

Set me whereas the sun doth parch the green,
Or where his beams may not dissolve the ice,
In temperate heat, where he is felt and seen;
With proud people, in presence sad and wise;
Set me in low, or yet in high degree;
In the long night, or in the shortest day;
In clear weather, or where clouds thickest be;
In lusty youth, or when my hairs be gray:
Set me in earth, in heaven, or yet in hell,
In hill, in dale, or in the foaming flood;
Thrall, or at large, alive whereso I dwell,
Sick, or in health, in ill fame or in good,
Yours will I be, and with this only thought
Comfort myself when that my hope is nought.

HENRY HOWARD: EARL OF SURREY
The Cornet

I never saw you, madam, lay apart
Your cornet black, in cold nor yet in heat,
Sith first ye knew of my desire so great
Which other fancies chas'd clean from my heart.
Whiles to myself I did the thought reserve
That so unware did wound my woeful breast,
Pity I saw within your heart did rest:
But since ye knew I did you love and serve
Your golden treese was clad always in black,
Your smiling looks were hid thus evermore,
All that withdrawn that I did crave so sore.
So doth this cornet govern me, alack,
In summer sun, in winter breath of frost,
Of your fair eyes whereby the light is lost.

HENRY HOWARD: EARL OF SURREY
The Pang

Alas, so all things now do hold their peace:
Heaven and earth disturbèd in no thing:
The beasts, the air, the birds their song do cease;
The nightès car the stars about doth bring.
Calm is the sea, the waves work less and less:
So am not I, whom love, alas, doth wring,
Bringing before my face the great increase
Of my desires, whereat I weep and sing
In joy and woe, as in a doubtful ease.
For my sweet thoughts sometime do pleasure bring,
But, by and by, the cause of my disease
Gives me a pang that inwardly doth sting,
When that I think what grief it is again
To live and lack the thing should rid my pain.

EDMUND SPENSER
From *Amoretti: VIII*

More than most fair, full of the living fire
Kindled above unto the Maker near:
No eyes but joys, in which all powers conspire
That to the world nought else be counted dear!
Through your bright beams doth not the blinded guest
Shoot out his dart to base affections wound;
But angels come to lead frail minds to rest
In chaste desires, on heavenly beauty bound.
You frame my thoughts, and fashion me within;
You stop my tongue, and teach my heart to speak;
You calm the storm that passion did begin,
Strong through your cause, but by your virtue weak.
Dark is the world where your light shinèd never;
Well is he born that may behold you ever.

EDMUND SPENSER
From *Amoretti: XXXIV*

Like as a ship that through the ocean wide,
By conduct of some star, doth make her way,
Whenas a storm hath dimmed her trusty guide,
Out of her course doth wander far astray, –
So I, whose star, that wont with her bright ray
Me to direct, with clouds is overcast,
Do wander now in darkness and dismay,
Through hidden perils round about me placed;
Yet hope I well that, when this storm is past,
My Helice, the lodestar of my life,
Will shine again, and look on me at last,
With lovely light to clear my cloudy grief.
Till then I wander careful, comfortless,
In secret sorrow and sad pensiveness.

EDMUND SPENSER
From *Amoretti: XXXVII*

What guile is this, that those her golden tresses
She doth attire under a net of gold;
And with sly skill so cunningly them dresses,
That which is gold or hair may scarce be told?
Is it that men's frail eyes which gaze too bold,
She may entangle in that golden snare;
And being caught may craftily enfold
Their weaker hearts which are not well aware?
Take heed therefore, mine eyes, how ye do stare
Henceforth too rashly on that guileful net,
In which if ever ye entrappèd are,
Out of her bands ye by no means shall get.
Fondness it were for any, being free,
To covet fetters, though they golden be!

EDMUND SPENSER
From *Amoretti: LXV*

The doubt which ye misdeem, fair Love, is vain,
That fondly fear to lose your liberty;
When losing one, two liberties ye gain,
And make him bond that bondage erst did fly.
Sweet be the bands the which true love doth tie
Without constraint or dread of any ill:
The gentle bird feels no captivity
Within her cage, but sings, and feeds her fill; –
There pride dare not approach, nor discord spill
The league 'twixt them that loyal love hath bound,
But simple truth and mutual good-will
Seeks with sweet peace to salve each other's wound;
There Faith doth fearless dwell in brazen tower,
And spotless Pleasure builds her sacred bower.

EDMUND SPENSER
From *Amoretti: LXVII*

Like as a huntsman after weary chase
Seeing the game from him escaped away,
Sits down to rest him in some shady place,
With panting hounds beguilèd of their prey, –
So, after long pursuit and vain assay,
When I all weary had the chase forsook,
The gentle deer returned the self-same way,
Thinking to quench her thirst at the next brook:
There she beholding me with milder look,
Sought not to fly, but fearless still did bide;
Till I in hand her yet half trembling took,
And with her own good-will her firmly tied.
Strange thing, me seemed, to see a beast so wild
So goodly won, with her own will beguiled.

EDMUND SPENSER
From *Amoretti: LXXV*

One day I wrote her name upon the strand;
But came the waves and washèd it away:
Again I wrote it with a second hand,
But came the tide and made my pains his prey.
Vain man! said she, that dost in vain assay
A mortal thing so to immortalize;
For I myself shall like to this decay,
And eke my name be wipèd out likewise.
Not so, quoth I; let baser things devise
To die in dust, but you shall live by fame:
My verse your virtues rare shall eternize,
And in the heavens write your glorious name, –
Where, whenas death shall all the world subdue,
Our love shall live, and later life renew.

EDMUND SPENSER
From *Amoretti: LXXIX*

Men call you fair, and you do credit it,
For that yourself ye daily such do see;
But the true fair, that is the gentle wit
And virtuous mind, is much more praised of me.
For all the rest, however fair it be,
Shall turn to nought and lose that glorious hue;
But only that is permanent and free
From frail corruption, that doth flesh ensue.
That is true beauty: that doth argue you
To be divine, and born of heavenly seed;
Derived from that fair Spirit from whom all true
And perfect beauty did at first proceed.
He only fair, and what He fair hath made;
All other fair, like flowers, untimely fade.

PHILIP SIDNEY
Absence

Finding those beams (which I must ever love)
To mar my mind, and with my hurt to please,
I deem'd it best some absence, for to prove
If farther place might further me to ease.
My eyes, thence drawn where livèd all their light,
Blinded forthwith in dark despair did lie,
Like to the mole, with want of guiding sight,
Deep plung'd in earth, deprivèd of the sky.
In absence blind, and wearied with that woe,
To greater woes, by presence, I return:
Even as the fly which to the flame doth go,
Pleas'd with the light that his small corse doth burn.
Fair choice I have, either to live or die:
A blinded mole, or else a burnèd fly.

PHILIP SIDNEY
A *Farewell*

Oft have I mused, but now at length I find,
Why those that die, men say they do depart.
Depart! – a word so gentle, to my mind,
Weakly did seem to paint Death's ougly dart.
But now the stars, with their strange course, do bind
Me one to leave, with whom I leave my heart:
I hear a cry of spirits faint and blind,
That, parting thus, my chiefest part I part.
Part of my life, the loathèd part to me,
Lives to impart my weary clay some breath:
But that good part, wherein all comforts be,
Now dead, doth show departure is a death –
Yea, worse than death: death parts both woe and joy:
From joy I part, still living in annoy.

PHILIP SIDNEY
From *Astrophel and Stella: I*

Loving in truth, and fain in verse my love to show,
That She, dear She, might take some pleasure of my
  pain,
Pleasure might cause her read, reading might make her
  know,
Knowledge might pity win, and pity grace obtain,
I sought fit words to paint the blackest face of woe;
Studying inventions fine, her wits to entertain,
Oft turning others' leaves, to see if thence would flow
Some fresh and fruitful showers upon my sun-burn'd
  brain.
But words came halting out, wanting Invention's stay;
Invention, Nature's child, fled stepdame Study's blows;
And others' feet still seem'd but strangers in my way.
Thus, great with child to speak, and helpless in my
  throes,
Biting my truand pen, beating myself for spite,
'Fool,' said my Muse to me, 'look in thy heart and
  write.'

PHILIP SIDNEY
From *Astrophel and Stella*: XIV

Alas, have I not pain enough, my friend,
Upon whose breast a fiercer grip doth tire
Than did on him who first stale down the fire,
While Love on me doth all his quiver spend?
But with your rhubarb words ye must contend
To grieve me worse, in saying that Desire
Doth plunge my well-form'd soul even in the mire
Of sinful thoughts, which do in ruin end.
If that be sin which doth the manners frame,
Well stay'd with truth in word and faith of deed,
Ready of wit, and fearing nought but shame;
If that be sin which in fixt hearts doth breed
A loathing of all loose unchastity –
Then love is sin, and let me sinful be.

PHILIP SIDNEY
From *Astrophel and Stella: XXXI*

With how sad steps, O Moon, thou climbst the skies!
How silently, and with how wan a face!
What, may it be that even in heavenly place
That busy archer his sharp arrows tries?
Sure, if that long-with-love-acquainted eyes
Can judge of love, thou feel'st a lover's case:
I read it in thy looks: thy languisht grace,
To me that feel the like, thy state descries.
Then even of fellowship, O Moon, tell me,
Is constant love deem'd there but want of wit?
Are beauties there as proud as here they be?
Do they above love to be lov'd, and yet
Those lovers scorn whom that love doth possess?
Do they call virtue there ungratefulness?

PHILIP SIDNEY
From *Astrophel and Stella: XXXIX*

Come, Sleep, O Sleep, the certain knot of peace,
The baiting-place of wit, the balm of woe,
The poor man's wealth, the prisoner's release,
The indifferent judge between the high and low!
With shield of proof shield me from out the prease
Of those fierce darts Despair at me doth throw.
O make in me those civil wars to cease:
I will good tribute pay, if thou do so.
Take thou of me smooth pillows, sweetest bed,
A chamber deaf of noise and blind of light,
A rosy garland and a weary head:
And if these things, as being thine in right,
Move not thy heavy grace, thou shalt in me,
Livelier than elsewhere, Stella's image see.

PHILIP SIDNEY
From *Astrophel and Stella: XLVII*

What, have I thus betray'd my liberty?
Can those black beams such burning marks engrave
In my free side, or am I born a slave,
Whose neck becomes such yoke of tyranny?
Or want I sense to feel my misery,
Or sprite, disdain of such disdain to have,
Who for long faith, tho' daily help I crave,
May get no alms but scorn of beggary?
Virtue, awake! Beauty but beauty is.
I may, I must, I can, I will, I do
Leave following that which it is gain to miss.
Let her go! Soft, but here she comes! Go to,
Unkind, I love you not! O me, that eye
Doth make my heart to give my tongue the lie!

PHILIP SIDNEY
From *Astrophel and Stella: LIV*

Because I breathe not love to every one,
Nor do not use set colours for to wear,
Nor nourish special locks of vowèd hair,
Nor give each speech a full point of a groan,
The courtly nymphs, acquainted with the moan
Of them which in their lips Love's standard bear,
'What, he!' say they of me, 'now I dare swear
He cannot love! No, no, let him alone.'
And think so still, so Stella know my mind;
Profess indeed I do not Cupid's art;
But you, fair maids, at length this true shall find,
That his right badge is but worn in the heart.
Dumb swans, not chattering pies, do lovers prove:
They love indeed who quake to say they love.

Oft with true sighs, oft with uncallèd tears,
Now with slow words, now with dumb eloquence,
I Stella's eyes assay'd, invade her ears;
But this, at last, is her sweet-breath'd defence:
That who indeed in-felt affection bears
So captives to his saint both soul and sense
That, wholly hers, all selfness he forbears,
Then his desires he learns, his life's course thence.
Now, since her chaste mind hates this love in me;
With chastened mind I straight must show that she
Shall quickly me from what she hates remove.
O Doctor Cupid, thou for me reply;
Driven else to grant, by angel's sophistry,
That I love not without I leave to love.

PHILIP SIDNEY
From *Astrophel and Stella: LXXIII*

Love still a boy and oft a wanton is,
School'd only by his mother's tender eye:
What wonder then if he his lesson miss,
When for so soft a rod dear play he try?
And yet my Star, because a sugared kiss
In sport I suckt while she asleep did lie,
Doth lower, nay chide, nay threat for only this.
Sweet, it was saucy Love, not humble I.
But no 'scuse serves. She makes her wrath appear
In Beauty's throne. See now, who dares come near
Those scarlet judges threatening bloody pain?
O heavenly fool, thy most kiss-worthy face
Anger invests with such a lovely grace
That Anger's self I needs must kiss again.

PHILIP SIDNEY
From *Astrophel and Stella: LXXIV*

I never drank of Aganippe well,
Nor ever did in shade of Tempe sit,
And Muses scorn with vulgar brains to dwell;
Poor layman I, for sacred rites unfit.
Some do I hear of poets' fury tell,
But, God wot, wot not what they mean by it;
And this I swear by blackest brook of hell,
I am no pick-purse of another's wit.
How falls it then, that with so smooth an ease
My thoughts I speak, and what I speak doth flow
In verse, and that my verse best wits doth please?
Guess we the cause? What, is it this? Fie, no.
Or so? Much less. How then? Sure thus it is:
My lips are sweet, inspired with Stella's kiss.

PHILIP SIDNEY
From *Astrophel and Stella: LXXXIV*

Highway, since you my chief Parnassus be,
And that my Muse, to some ears not unsweet,
Tempers her words to trampling horses' feet
More oft than to a chamber-melody,
Now, blessed you, bear onward blessed me
To her where I my heart, safe-left, shall meet:
My Muse and I must you of duty greet
With thanks and wishes, wishing thankfully.
Be you still careful kept by public heed,
By no encroachment wrong'd, nor time forgot,
Nor blamed for blood, nor shamed for sinful deed,
And, that you know I envy you no lot
Of highest wish, I wish you so much bliss,
Hundreds of years you Stella's feet may kiss!

PHILIP SIDNEY
From *Astrophel and Stella*: XC

Stella, think not that I by verse seek fame
Who seek, who hope, who love, who live but thee;
Thine eyes my pride, thy lips mine history:
If thou praise not, all other praise is shame.
Not so ambitious am I as to frame
A nest for my young praise in laurel tree:
In truth I swear, I wish not there should be
Graved in my epitaph a poet's name.
Ne, if I would, could I just title make,
That any laud thereof to me should grow,
Without my plumes from others' wings I take:
For nothing from my wit or will doth flow,
Since all my words thy beauty doth indite,
And Love doth hold my hand and makes me write.

SAMUEL DANIEL
From *Delia: IX*

If this be love, to draw a weary breath,
Paint on floods, till the shore, cry to th'air;
With downward looks, still reading on the earth
The sad memorials of my love's despair.
If this be love, to war against my soul,
Lie down to wail, rise up to sigh and grieve me,
The never-resting stone of care to roll,
Still to complain my griefs, and none relieve me;
If this be love, to clothe me with dark thoughts,
Haunting untrodden paths to wail apart;
My pleasures horror, music tragic notes,
Tears in my eyes, and sorrow at my heart.
If this be love, to live a living death,
O then love I, and draw this weary breath.

SAMUEL DANIEL
From *Delia: XXXI*

Look, Delia, how we esteem the half-blown rose,
The image of thy blush, and summer's honour,
Whilst in her tender green she doth enclose
That pure sweet beauty Time bestows upon her.
No sooner spreads her glory in the air,
But straight her full-blown pride is in declining;
She then is scorned that late adorned the fair;
So clouds thy beauty after fairest shining.
No April can revive thy withered flowers,
Whose blooming grace adorns thy glory now;
Swift speedy Time, feathered with flying hours,
Dissolves the beauty of the fairest brow.
O let not then such riches waste in vain,
But love whilst that thou mayest be loved again.

MICHAEL DRAYTON
From *Idea: VI*

How many paltry, foolish, painted things,
That now in coaches trouble ev'ry street,
Shall be forgotten, whom no poet sings,
Ere they be well wrapp'd in their winding-sheet?
Where I to thee eternity shall give,
When nothing else remaineth of these days,
And queens hereafter shall be glad to live
Upon the alms of thy superfluous praise;
Virgins and matrons reading these my rhymes,
Shall be so much delighted with thy story,
That they shall grieve they liv'd not in these times,
To have seen thee, their sex's only glory:
  So shalt thou fly above the vulgar throng,
  Still to survive in my immortal song.

MICHAEL DRAYTON
From *Idea: LXI*

Since there's no help, come let us kiss and part,
Nay, I have done: you get no more of me,
And I am glad, yea, glad with all my heart,
That thus so cleanly I myself can free,
Shake hands for ever, cancel all our vows,
And when we meet at any time again,
Be it not seen in either of our brows,
That we one jot of former love retain;
Now at the last gasp, of love's latest breath,
When, his pulse failing, passion speechless lies,
When faith is kneeling by his bed of death,
And innocence is closing up his eyes,
   Now if thou would'st, when all have given him
   over,
   From death to life, thou might'st him yet recover.

JOHN LILY
Sonnet

Cupid and my Campaspe played
At cards for kisses, Cupid paid;
He stakes his quiver, bow, and arrows,
His mother's doves, and team of sparrows;
Loses them too; then, down he throws
The coral of his lip, the rose
Growing on's cheek (but none knows how);
With these, the crystal of his brow,
And then the dimple of his chin:
All these did my Campaspe win.
At last, he set her both his eyes;
She won, and Cupid blind did rise.

    O Love! has she done this to thee?
    What shall (alas!) become of me?

HENRY CONSTABLE
Sonnet

My lady's presence makes the roses red
Because to see her lips they blush for shame;
The lily's leaves, for envy, pale became,
For her white hands in them this envy bred.
The marigold the leaves abroad doth spread,
Because the sun's and her power is the same
The violet of purple colour came,
Dyed in the blood she made my heart to shed.
In brief, all flowers from her their virtue take;
From her sweet breath their sweet smells do proceed;
The living heat which her eyebeams do make
Warmeth the ground, and quickeneth the seed.
The rain, wherewith she watereth the flowers,
Falls from mine eyes, which she dissolves in showers.

WILLIAM DRUMMOND
Sonnet

I know that all beneath the moon decays,
And what by mortals in this world is brought,
In Time's great periods shall return to nought;
That fairest states have fatal nights and days;
I know how all the Muse's heavenly lays,
With toil of spright which are so dearly bought,
As idle sounds of few or none are sought,
And that nought lighter is than airy praise.
I know frail beauty like the purple flower,
To which one morn oft birth and death affords;
That love a jarring is of minds' accords,
Where sense and will invassal reason's power:
Know what I list, this all can not me move,
But that, O me! I both must write and love.

WILLIAM SHAKESPEARE
Sonnet XVIII

Shall I compare thee to a summer's day?
Thou art more lovely and more temperate.
Rough winds do shake the darling buds of May,
And summer's lease hath all too short a date.
Sometime too hot the eye of heaven shines,
And often is his gold complexion dimmed;
And every fair from fair sometime declines,
By chance, or nature's changing course, untrimmed:
But thy eternal summer shall not fade
Nor lose possession of that fair thou ow'st,
Nor shall Death brag thou wand'rest in his shade
When in eternal lines to time thou grow'st.
  So long as men can breathe or eyes can see,
  So long lives this, and this gives life to thee.

WILLIAM SHAKESPEARE
Sonnet XXIX

When, in disgrace with Fortune and men's eyes,
I all alone beweep my outcast state,
And trouble deaf heaven with my bootless cries,
And look upon myself and curse my fate,
Wishing me like to one more rich in hope,
Featured like him, like him with friends possessed,
Desiring this man's art, and that man's scope,
With what I most enjoy contented least;
Yet in these thoughts myself almost despising,
Haply I think on thee, and then my state,
Like to the lark at break of day arising
From sullen earth, sings hymns at heaven's gate;
    For thy sweet love rememb'red such wealth brings
    That then I scorn to change my state with kings.

WILLIAM SHAKESPEARE
Sonnet XXX

When to the sessions of sweet silent thought
I summon up remembrance of things past,
I sigh the lack òf many a thing I sought,
And with old woes new wail my dear time's waste:
Then can I drown an eye, unused to flow,
For precious friends hid in death's dateless night,
And weep afresh love's long since cancelled woe,
And moan th' expense of many a vanished sight.
Then can I grieve at grievances foregone,
And heavily from woe to woe tell o'er
The sad account of fore-bemoanèd moan,
Which I new pay as if not paid before.
    But if the while I think on thee, dear friend,
    All losses are restored and sorrows end.

WILLIAM SHAKESPEARE
Sonnet LXXI

No longer mourn for me when I am dead
Than you shall hear the surly sullen bell
Give warning to the world that I am fled
From this vile world, with vilest worms to dwell.
Nay, if you read this line, remember not
The hand that writ it, for I love you so
That I in your sweet thoughts would be forgot
If thinking on me then should make you woe.
O, if, I say, you look upon this verse
When I, perhaps, compounded am with clay,
Do not so much as my poor name rehearse,
But let your love even with my life decay,
　Lest the wise world should look into your moan
　And mock you with me after I am gone.

WILLIAM SHAKESPEARE
Sonnet LXXIII

That time of year thou mayst in me behold
When yellow leaves, or none, or few, do hang
Upon those boughs which shake against the cold,
Bare ruined choirs where late the sweet birds sang.
In me thou seest the twilight of such day
As after sunset fadeth in the west,
Which by and by black night doth take away,
Death's second self that seals up all in rest.
In me thou seest the glowing of such fire
That on the ashes of his youth doth lie,
As the deathbed whereon it must expire,
Consumed with that which it was nourished by.
   This thou perceiv'st, which makes thy love more
   strong,
   To love that well which thou must leave ere long.

WILLIAM SHAKESPEARE
Sonnet LXXXVII

Farewell: thou art too dear for my possessing,
And like enough thou know'st thy estimate.
The charter of thy worth gives thee releasing;
My bonds in thee are all determinate.
For how do I hold thee but by thy granting,
And for that riches where is my deserving?
The cause of this fair gift in me is wanting,
And so my patent back again is swerving.
Thyself thou gav'st, thy own worth then not knowing,
Or me, to whom thou gav'st it, else mistaking;
So thy great gift, upon misprision growing,
Comes home again, on better judgement making.
  Thus have I had thee as a dream doth flatter,
    In sleep a king, but waking no such matter.

WILLIAM SHAKESPEARE
Sonnet XC

Then hate me when thou wilt; if ever, now;
Now, while the world is bent my deeds to cross,
Join with the spite of fortune, make me bow,
And do not drop in for an after-loss.
Ah, do not, when my heart hath scaped this sorrow,
Come in the rearward of a conquered woe;
Give not a windy night a rainy morrow,
To linger out a purposed overthrow.
If thou wilt leave me, do not leave me last,
When other petty griefs have done their spite,
But in the onset come: so shall I taste
At first the very worst of fortune's might;
   And other strains of woe, which now seem woe,
   Compared with loss of thee will not seem so.

WILLIAM SHAKESPEARE
Sonnet XCIV

They that have pow'r to hurt and will do none,
That do not do the thing they most do show,
Who, moving others, are themselves as stone,
Unmovèd, cold, and to temptation slow;
They rightly do inherit heaven's graces
And husband nature's riches from expense;
They are the lords and owners of their faces.
Others but stewards of their excellence.
The summer's flow'r is to the summer sweet,
Though to itself it only live and die;
But if that flow'r with base infection meet,
The basest weed outbraves his dignity:
   For sweetest things turn sourest by their deeds;
   Lilies that fester smell far worse than weeds.

WILLIAM SHAKESPEARE
Sonnet XCVII

How like a winter hath my absence been
From thee, the pleasure of the fleeting year!
What freezings have I felt, what dark days seen!
What old December's bareness everywhere!
And yet this time removed was summer's time,
The teeming autumn, big with rich increase,
Bearing the wanton burden of the prime,
Like widowed wombs after their lords' decease:
Yet this abundant issue seemed to me
But hope of orphans and unfathered fruit;
For summer and his pleasures wait on thee,
And, thou away, the very birds are mute;
   Or, if they sing, 'tis with so dull a cheer
   That leaves look pale, dreading the winter's near.

WILLIAM SHAKESPEARE
Sonnet CIV

To me, fair friend, you never can be old,
For as you were when first your eye I eyed,
Such seems your beauty still. Three winters cold
Have from the forests shook three summers' pride,
Three beauteous springs to yellow autumn turned
In process of the seasons have I seen,
Three April perfumes in three hot Junes burned,
Since first I saw you fresh, which yet are green.
Ah, yet doth beauty, like a dial hand,
Steal from his figure, and no pace perceived;
So your sweet hue, which methinks still doth stand,
Hath motion, and mine eye may be deceived;
   For fear of which, hear this, thou age unbred:
   Ere you were born was beauty's summer dead.

WILLIAM SHAKESPEARE
Sonnet CIX

O, never say that I was false of heart,
Though absence seemed my flame to qualify;
As easy might I from myself depart
As from my soul, which in thy breast doth lie.
That is my home of love: if I have ranged,
Like him that travels I return again,
Just to the time, not with the time exchanged,
So that myself bring water for my stain.
Never believe, though in my nature reigned
All frailties that besiege all kinds of blood,
That it could so preposterously be stained
To leave for nothing all thy sum of good;
   For nothing this wide universe I call
   Save thou, my rose; in it thou art my all.

WILLIAM SHAKESPEARE
Sonnet CXVI

Let me not to the marriage of true minds
Admit impediments; love is not love
Which alters when it alteration finds
Or bends with the remover to remove.
O, no, it is an ever-fixèd mark
That looks on tempests and is never shaken;
It is the star to every wand'ring bark,
Whose worth's unknown, although his height be
    taken.
Love's not Time's fool, though rosy lips and cheeks
Within his bending sickle's compass come;
Love alters not with his brief hours and weeks,
But bears it out even to the edge of doom.
    If this be error, and upon me proved,
    I never writ, nor no man ever loved.

WILLIAM SHAKESPEARE
Sonnet CXXIX

Th' expense of spirit in a waste of shame
Is lust in action; and, till action, lust
Is perjured, murd'rous, bloody, full of blame,
Savage, extreme, rude, cruel, not to trust;
Enjoyed no sooner but despisèd straight;
Past reason hunted, and no sooner had,
Past reason hated as a swallowed bait
On purpose laid to make the taker mad:
Mad in pursuit, and in possession so;
Had, having, and in quest to have, extreme;
A bliss in proof, and proved, a very woe;
Before, a joy proposed; behind, a dream.
  All this the world well knows; yet none knows well
  To shun the heaven that leads men to this hell.

WILLIAM SHAKESPEARE
Sonnet CLI

Love is too young to know what conscience is;
Yet who knows not conscience is born of love?
Then, gentle cheater, urge not my amiss,
Lest guilty of my faults thy sweet self prove.
For, thou betraying me, I do betray
My nobler part to my gross body's treason;
My soul doth tell my body that he may
Triumph in love; flesh stays no farther reason,
But, rising at thy name, doth point out thee
As his triumphant prize. Proud of this pride,
He is contented thy poor drudge to be,
To stand in thy affairs, fall by thy side.
   No want of conscience hold it that I call
   Her 'love' for whose dear love I rise and fall.

WILLIAM SHAKESPEARE
Sonnet CLII

In loving thee thou know'st I am forsworn,
But thou art twice forsworn, to me love swearing;
In act thy bed-vow broke, and new faith torn
In vowing new hate after new love bearing.
But why of two oaths' breach do I accuse thee
When I break twenty? I am perjured most,
For all my vows are oaths but to misuse thee,
And all my honest faith in thee is lost;
For I have sworn deep oaths of thy deep kindness,
Oaths of thy love, thy truth, thy constancy;
And, to enlighten thee, gave eyes to blindness,
Or made them swear against the thing they see;
    For I have sworn thee fair; more perjured eye,
    To swear against the truth so foul a lie.

THOMAS CAREW
To My Inconstant Mistris

When thou, poore excommunicate
  From all the joyes of love, shalt see
The full reward, and glorious fate,
  Which my strong faith shall purchase me,
  Then curse thine owne inconstancie.

A fayrer hand than thine, shall cure
  That heart, which thy false oathes did wound;
And to my soule, a soule more pure
  Than thine, shall by Loves hand be bound,
  And both with equall glory crown'd.

Then shalt thou weepe, entreat, complaine
  To Love, as I did once to thee;
When all thy teares shall be as vaine
  As mine were then, for thou shalt bee
Damn'd for thy false Apostasie.

THOMAS CAREW
Mediocritie in Love Rejected

Give me more love, or more disdaine;
   The Torrid, or the frozen Zonc,
Bring equall ease unto my paine;
   The temperate affords me none:
Either extreme, of love, or hate,
Is sweeter than a calm estate.

Give me a storme; if it be love,
   Like *Danae* in that golden showre
I swimme in pleasure; if it prove
   Disdaine, that torrent will devoure
My Vulture-hopes; and he's possest
Of Heaven, that's but from Hell releast:
   Then crowne my joyes, or cure my paine;
   Give me more love, or more disdaine.

THOMAS CAREW
Red and White Roses

Read in these Roses the sad story
Of my hard fate, and your owne glory.
In the White you may discover
The paleness of a fainting lover;
In the Red the flames still feeding
On my heart, with fresh wounds bleeding.
The White will tell you how I languish,
And the Red express my anguish;
The White my innocence displaying,
The Red my martyrdom betraying.
The frowns that on your brow resided,
Have those Roses thus divided.
Oh! let your smiles but clear the weather,
And then they both shall grow together.

JOHN MILTON
Sonnet

Methought I saw my late espoused saint
   Brought to me like Alcestis from the grave,
   Whom Jove's great son to her glad husband gave,
   Rescued from death by force, though pale and faint.
Mine, as whom washed from spot of childbed taint
   Purification in the old Law did save,
   And such as yet once more I trust to have
   Full sight of her in heaven without restraint,
Came vested all in white, pure as her mind.
   Her face was veiled, yet to my fancied sight
   Love, sweetness, goodness, in her person shined
So clear as in no face with more delight.
   But O as to embrace me she inclined,
   I waked, she fled, and day brought back my night.

WILLIAM WORDSWORTH
Sonnet

Surprised by joy – impatient as the wind
I turned to share the transport – Oh! with whom
But thee, deep buried in the silent tomb,
That spot which no vicissitude can find?
Love, faithful love, recalled thee to my mind –
But how could I forget thee? Through what power,
Even for the least division of an hour,
Have I been so beguiled as to be blind
To my most grievous loss! – That thought's return
Was the worst pang that sorrow ever bore,
Save one, one only, when I stood forlorn,
Knowing my heart's best treasure was no more;
That neither present time, nor years unborn
Could to my sight that heavenly face restore.

JOHN KEATS
Sonnet

Bright star, would I were stedfast as thou art –
Not in lone splendour hung aloft the night
And watching, with eternal lids apart,
Like nature's patient, sleepless Eremite,
The moving waters at their priestlike task
Of pure ablution round earth's human shores,
Or gazing on the new soft fallen mask
Of snow upon the mountains and the moors –
No – yet still stedfast, still unchangeable,
Pillow'd upon my fair love's ripening breast,
To feel forever its soft fall and swell,
Awake forever in a sweet unrest,
Still, still to hear her tender-taken breath,
And so live ever – or else swoon to death.

JOHN KEATS
To Fanny

I cry your mercy – pity – love! – ay, love! –
Merciful love that tantalizes not,
One-thoughted, never-wandering, guileless love,
Unmask'd, and being seen – without a blot!
O! let me have thee whole – all – all – be mine!
That shape, that fairness, that sweet minor zest
Of love, your kiss – those hands, those eyes divine,
That warm, white, lucent, million-pleasured breast –
Yourself – your soul – in pity give me all,
Withhold no atom's atom or I die,
Or living on perhaps, your wretched thrall,
Forget, in the midst of idle misery,
Life's purposes – the palate of my mind
Losing its gust, and my ambition blind!

ELIZABETH BARRETT BROWNING
From *Sonnets from the Portuguese: 1*

I thought once how Theocritus had sung
Of the sweet years, the dear and wished-for years,
Who each one in a gracious hand appears
To bear a gift for mortals, old or young:
And, as I mused it in his antique tongue,
I saw, in gradual vision through my tears,
The sweet, sad years, the melancholy years,
Those of my own life, who by turns had flung
A shadow across me. Straightway I was 'ware,
So weeping, how a mystic Shape did move
Behind me, and drew me backward by the hair,
And a voice said in mastery while I strove, . . .
'Guess now who holds thee?' – 'Death,' I said. But,
   there,
The silver answer rang, . . . 'Not Death, but Love.'

ELIZABETH BARRETT BROWNING
From *Sonnets from the Portuguese: VI*

Go from me. Yet I feel that I shall stand
Henceforward in thy shadow. Nevermore
Alone upon the threshold of my door
Of individual life, I shall command
The uses of my soul, nor lift my hand
Serenely in the sunshine as before,
Without the sense of that which I forbore, . . .
Thy touch upon the palm. The widest land
Doom takes to part us, leaves thy heart in mine
With pulses that beat double. What I do
And what I dream include thee, as the wine
Must taste of its own grapes. And when I sue
God for myself, He hears that name of thine,
And sees within my eyes the tears of two.

ELIZABETH BARRETT BROWNING
From *Sonnets from the Portuguese: IX*

Can it be right to give what I can give?
To let thee sit beneath the fall of tears
As salt as mine, and hear the sighing years
Re-sighing on my lips renunciative
Through those infrequent smiles which fail to live
For all thy adjurations? O my fears,
That this can scarce be right! We are not peers,
So to be lovers; and I own, and grieve,
That givers of such gifts as mine are, must
Be counted with the ungenerous. Out, alas!
I will not soil thy purple with my dust,
Nor breathe my poison on thy Venice-glass,
Nor give thee any love . . . which were unjust.
Beloved, I only love thee! let it pass.

ELIZABETH BARRETT BROWNING
From *Sonnets from the Portuguese: XIV*

If thou must love me, let it be for nought
Except for love's sake only. Do not say
'I love her for her smile . . . her look . . . her way
Of speaking gently, . . . for a trick of thought
That falls in well with mine, and certes brought
A sense of pleasant ease on such a day' –
For these things in themselves, Belovèd, may
Be changed, or change for thee, – and love, so
    wrought,
May be unwrought so. Neither love me for
Thine own dear pity's wiping my cheeks dry, –
A creature might forget to weep, who bore
Thy comfort long, and lose thy love thereby!
But love me for love's sake, that evermore
Thou mayst love on, through love's eternity.

ELIZABETH BARRETT BROWNING
From *Sonnets from the Portuguese*: XVIII

I never gave a lock of hair away
To a man, dearest, except this to thee,
Which now upon my fingers thoughtfully
I ring out to the full brown length and say
'Take it.' My day of youth went yesterday;
My hair no longer bounds to my foot's glee,
Nor plant I it from rose or myrtle-tree,
As girls do, any more. It only may
Now shade on two pale cheeks, the mark of tears,
Taught drooping from the head that hangs aside
Through sorrow's trick. I thought the funeral-shears
Would take this first, but Love is justified, –
Take it, thou, . . . finding pure, from all those years,
The kiss my mother left here when she died.

ELIZABETH BARRETT BROWNING
From *Sonnets from the Portuguese: XXII*

When our two souls stand up erect and strong,
Face to face, silent, drawing nigh and nigher,
Until the lengthening wings break into fire
At either curvèd point, – what bitter wrong
Can the earth do to us, that we should not long
Be here contented? Think. In mounting higher,
The angels would press on us, and aspire
To drop some golden orb of perfect song
Into our deep, dear silence. Let us stay
Rather on earth, Belovèd, – where the unfit
Contrarious moods of men recoil away
And isolate pure spirits, and permit
A place to stand and love in for a day,
With darkness and the death-hour rounding it.

ELIZABETH BARRETT BROWNING
From *Sonnets from the Portuguese: XXXII*

The first time that the sun rose on thine oath
To love me, I looked forward to the moon
To slacken all those bonds which seemed too soon
And quickly tied to make a lasting troth.
Quick-loving hearts, I thought, may quickly loathe;
And, looking on myself, I seemed not one
For such man's love! – more like an out of tune
Worn viol, a good singer would be wroth
To spoil his song with, and which, snatched in haste,
Is laid down at the first ill-sounding note.
I did not wrong myself so, but I placed
A wrong on *thee*. For perfect strains may float
'Neath master-hands, from instruments defaced, –
And great souls, at one stroke, may do and dote.

ELIZABETH BARRETT BROWNING
From *Sonnets from the Portuguese: XXXV*

If I leave all for thee, wilt thou exchange
And be all to me? Shall I never miss
Home-talk and blessing and the common kiss
That comes to each in turn, nor count it strange,
When I look up, to drop on a new range
Of walls and floors . . . another home than this?
Nay, wilt thou fill that place by me which is
Filled by dead eyes too tender to know change?
That's hardest. If to conquer love, has tried,
To conquer grief, tries more . . . as all things prove;
For grief indeed is love and grief beside.
Alas, I have grieved so I am hard to love.
Yet love me – wilt thou? Open thine heart wide,
And fold within, the wet wings of thy dove.

ELIZABETH BARRETT BROWNING
From *Sonnets from the Portuguese: XLIII*

How do I love thee? Let me count the ways.
I love thee to the depth and breadth and height
My soul can reach, when feeling out of sight.
For the ends of Being and ideal Grace.
I love thee to the level of every day's
Most quiet need, by sun and candlelight.
I love thee freely, as men strive for Right;
I love thee purely, as they turn from Praise.
I love thee with the passion put to use
In my old griefs, and with my childhood's faith.
I love thee with a love I seemed to lose
With my lost saints, – I love thee with the breath,
Smiles, tears, of all my life! – and, if God choose,
I shall but love thee better after death.

ELIZABETH BARRETT BROWNING
From *Sonnets from the Portuguese: XLIV*

Belovèd, thou hast brought me many flowers
Plucked in the garden, all the summer through
And winter, and it seemed as if they grew
In this close room, nor missed the sun and showers.
So, in the like name of that love of ours,
Take back these thoughts which here unfolded too,
And which on warm and cold days I withdrew
From my heart's ground. Indeed, those beds and
    bowers
Be overgrown with bitter weeds and rue,
And wait thy weeding; yet here's eglantine,
Here's ivy! – take them, as I used to do
Thy flowers, and keep them where they shall not pine.
Instruct thine eyes to keep their colours true,
And tell thy soul, their roots are left in mine.

CHRISTINA ROSSETTI
Remember

Remember me when I am gone away,
   Gone far away into the silent land;
   When you can no more hold me by the hand,
Nor I half turn to go yet turning stay.
Remember me when no more day by day
   You tell me of our future that you planned:
   Only remember me; you understand
It will be late to counsel then or pray.
Yet if you should forget me for a while
   And afterwards remember, do not grieve:
   For if the darkness and corruption leave
   A vestige of the thoughts that once I had,
Better by far you should forget and smile
   Than that you should remember and be sad.

CHRISTINA ROSSETTI
Autumn Violets

Keep love for youth, and violets for the spring:
  Or if these bloom when worn-out autumn grieves,
  Let them lie hid in double shade of leaves,
Their own, and others dropped down withering;
For violets suit when home birds build and sing,
  Not when the outbound bird a passage cleaves;
  Not with dry stubble of mown harvest sheaves,
But when the green world buds to blossoming.
Keep violets for the spring, and love for youth,
  Love that should dwell with beauty, mirth, and
    hope:
    Or if a later sadder love be born,
    Let this not look for grace beyond its scope,
But give itself, nor plead for answering truth –
    A grateful Ruth tho' gleaning scanty corn.

CHRISTINA ROSSETTI
From *Monna Innominata: I*

Come back to me, who wait and watch for you: –
    Or come not yet, for it is over then,
    And long it is before you come again,
So far between my pleasures are and few.
While, when you come not, what I do I do
    Thinking 'Now when he comes,' my sweetest 'when:'
    For one man is my world of all the men
This wide world holds; O love, my world is you.
Howbeit, to meet you grows almost a pang
    Because the pang of parting comes so soon;
My hope hangs waning, waxing, like a moon
    Between the heavenly days on which we meet:
Ah me, but where are now the songs I sang
    When life was sweet because you called them sweet?

CHRISTINA ROSSETTI
From *Monna Innominata: II*

I wish I could remember that first day,
   First hour, first moment of your meeting me,
   If bright or dim the season, it might be
Summer or Winter for aught I can say;
So unrecorded did it slip away,
   So blind was I to see and to foresee,
   So dull to mark the budding of my tree
That would not blossom yet for many a May.
If only I could recollect it, such
   A day of days! I let it come and go
   As traceless as a thaw of bygone snow;
It seemed to mean so little, meant so much;
If only now I could recall that touch,
   First touch of hand in hand – Did one but know!

CHRISTINA ROSSETTI
From *Monna Innominata: III*

I dream of you to wake: would that I might
  Dream of you and not wake but slumber on;
  Nor find with dreams the dear companion gone,
As Summer ended Summer birds take flight.
In happy dreams I hold you full in sight,
  I blush again who waking look so wan;
  Brighter than sunniest day that ever shone,
In happy dreams your smile makes day of night.
Thus only in a dream we are at one,
  Thus only in a dream we give and take
    The faith that maketh rich who take or give;
  If thus to sleep is sweeter than to wake,
    To die were surely sweeter than to live,
Tho' there be nothing new beneath the sun.

CHRISTINA ROSSETTI
From *Monna Innominata: IV*

I loved you first: but afterwards your love
  Outsoaring mine, sang such a loftier song
As drowned the friendly cooings of my dove.
  Which owes the other most? my love was long,
  And yours one moment seemed to wax more strong;
I loved and guessed at you, you construed me
And loved me for what might or might not be –
  Nay, weights and measures do us both a wrong.
For verily love knows not 'mine' or 'thine;'
  With separate 'I' and 'thou' free love has done,
    For one is both and both are one in love:
Rich love knows nought of 'thine that is not mine;'
  Both have the strength and both the length
  thereof,
    Both of us, of the love which makes us one.

CHRISTINA ROSSETTI
From *Monna Innominata: IX*

Thinking of you, and all that was, and all
   That might have been and now can never be,
   I feel your honoured excellence, and see
Myself unworthy of the happier call:
For woe is me who walk so apt to fall,
   So apt to shrink afraid, so apt to flee,
   Apt to lie down and die (ah, woe is me!)
Faithless and hopeless turning to the wall.
And yet not hopeless quite nor faithless quite,
Because not loveless; love may toil all night,
   But take at morning; wrestle till the break
      Of day, but then wield power with God and
man: –
      So take I heart of grace as best I can,
    Ready to spend and be spent for your sake.

CHRISTINA ROSSETTI
From *Monna Innominata: XI*

Many in aftertimes will say of you
  'He loved her' – while of me what will they say?
  Not that I loved you more than just in play,
For fashion's sake as idle women do.
Even let them prate; who know not what we knew
  Of love and parting in exceeding pain.
  Of parting hopeless here to meet again,
Hopeless on earth, and heaven is out of view.
But by my heart of love laid bare to you.
  My love that you can make not void nor vain,
Love that foregoes you but to claim anew
    Beyond this passage of the gate of death,
  I charge you at the Judgment make it plain
    My love of you was life and not a breath.

CHRISTINA ROSSETTI
From *Monna Innominata: XII*

If there be any one can take my place
   And make you happy whom I grieve to grieve,
   Think not that I can grudge it, but believe
I do commend you to that nobler grace,
That readier wit than mine, that sweeter face;
   Yea, since your riches make me rich, conceive
   I too am crowned, while bridal crowns I weave,
And thread the bridal dance with jocund pace.
For if I did not love you, it might be
   That I should grudge you some one dear delight;
     But since the heart is yours that was mine own,
    Your pleasure is my pleasure, right my right,
   Your honourable freedom makes me free,
      And you companioned I am not alone.

CHRISTINA ROSSETTI
From *Monna Innominata: XIV*

Youth gone, and beauty gone if ever there
   Dwelt beauty in so poor a face as this;
   Youth gone and beauty, what remains of bliss?
I will not bind fresh roses in my hair,
To shame a cheek at best but little fair, –
   Leave youth his roses, who can bear a thorn, –
I will not seek for blossoms anywhere,
   Except such common flowers as blow with corn.
Youth gone and beauty gone, what doth remain?
   The longing of a heart pent up forlorn,
     A silent heart whose silence loves and longs;
     The silence of a heart which sang its songs
   While youth and beauty make a summer morn,
Silence of love that cannot sing again.

GEORGE MEREDITH
From *Modern Love: L*

Thus piteously Love closed what he begat:
The union of this ever-diverse pair!
These two were rapid falcons in a snare,
Condemned to do the flitting of the bat.
Lovers beneath the singing sky of May,
They wandered once; clear as the dew on flowers:
But they fed not on the advancing hours:
Their hearts held cravings for the buried day.
Then each applied to each that fatal knife,
Deep questioning, which probes to endless dole.
Ah, what a dusty answer gets the soul
When hot for certainties in this our life! –
In tragic hints here see what evermore
Moves dark as yonder midnight ocean's force,
Thundering like ramping hosts of warrior horse,
To throw that faint thin line upon the shore!

GEORGE MEREDITH
From *Modern Love: XLVII*

We saw the swallows gathering in the sky,
And in the osier-isle we heard them noise.
We had not to look back on summer joys,
Or forward to a summer of bright dye:
But in the largeness of the evening earth
Our spirits grew as we went side by side.
The hour became her husband and my bride.
Love, that had robbed us so, thus blessed our dearth!
The pilgrims of the year waxed very loud
In multitudinous chatterings, as the flood
Full brown came from the West, and like pale blood
Expanded to the upper crimson cloud.
Love, that had robbed us of immortal things,
This little moment mercifully gave,
Where I have seen across the twilight wave
The swan sail with her young beneath her wings.

DANTE GABRIEL ROSSETTI
Silent Noon

Your hands lie open in the long fresh grass,
The finger-points look through like rosy blooms;
Your eyes smile peace. The pasture gleams and glooms
'Neath billowing skies that scatter and amass.
All round our nest, far as the eye can pass,
Are golden kingcup-fields with silver edge
Where the cow-parsley skirts the hawthorn-hedge.
'Tis visible silence still as the hourglass.
Deep in the sun-searched growths the dragonfly
Hangs like a blue thread loosened from the sky.
So this winged hour is dropt to us from above
Oh! clasp we to our hearts, for deathless dower,
This close-companioned inarticulate hour
When twofold silence was the song of love.

DANTE GABRIEL ROSSETTI
Willow-wood

I sat with Love upon a woodside well,
Leaning across the water, I and he;
Nor ever did he speak nor looked at me,
But touched his lute wherein was audible
The certain secret thing he had to tell:
Only our mirrored eyes met silently
In the low wave; and that sound seemed to be
The passionate voice I knew; and my tears fell.

And at their fall, his eyes beneath grew hers;
And with his foot and with his wing feathers
He swept the spring that watered my heart's drouth.
Then the dark ripples spread to waving hair,
And as I stopped, her own lips rising there
Bubbled with brimming kisses at my mouth.

DANTE GABRIEL ROSSETTI
Without Her

What of her glass without her? The blank grey
  There where the pool is blind of the moon's face.
  Her dress without her? The tossed empty space
Of cloud-rack whence the moon has passed away.
Her paths without her? Day's appointed sway
  Usurped by desolate night. Her pillowed place
  Without her? Tears, ah me! for love's good grace,
And cold forgetfulness of night or day.

What of the heart without her? Nay, poor heart,
  Of thee what word remains ere speech be still?
  A wayfarer by barren ways and chill,
Steep ways and weary, without her thou art,
Where the long cloud, the long wood's counterpart,
  Sheds doubled darkness up the labouring hill.

A. C. SWINBURNE
Love and Sleep

Lying asleep between the strokes of night
   I saw my love lean over my sad bed,
   Pale as the duskiest lily's leaf or head,
Smooth-skinned and dark, with bare throat made to
   bite,
Too wan for blushing and too warm for white,
   But perfect-coloured without white or red.
   And her lips opened amorously, and said –
I wist not what, saving one word – Delight.

And all her face was honey to my mouth,
   And all her body pasture to mine eyes;
     The long lithe arms and hotter hands than fire,
The quivering flanks, hair smelling of the south,
   The bright light feet, the splendid supple thighs
     And glittering eyelids of my soul's desire.

ARTHUR SYMONS
Nerves

The modern malady of love is nerves.
Love, once a simple madness, now observes
The stages of his passionate disease,
And is twice sorrowful because he sees,
Inch by inch entering, the fatal knife.
O health of simple minds, give me your life,
And let me, for one midnight, cease to hear
The clock for ever ticking in my ear,
The clock that tells the minutes in my brain.
It is not love, nor love's despair, this pain
That shoots a witless, keener pang across
The simple agony of love and loss.
Nerves, nerves! O folly of a child who dreams
Of heaven, and, waking in the darkness, screams.

EDWARD THOMAS
Some Eyes Condemn

Some eyes condemn the earth they gaze upon:
Some wait patiently till they know far more
Than earth can tell them: some laugh at the whole
As folly of another's making: one
I knew that laughed because he saw, from core
To rind, not one thing worth the laugh his soul
Had ready at waking: some eyes have begun
With laughing; some stand startled at the door.

Others, too, I have seen rest, question, roll,
Dance, shoot. And many I have loved watching. Some
I could not take my eyes from till they turned
And loving died. I had not found my goal.
But thinking of your eyes, dear, I become
Dumb: for they flamed and it was me they burned.

RUPERT BROOKE
The Hill

Breathless, we flung us on the windy hill,
  Laughed in the sun, and kissed the lovely grass.
  You said, 'Through glory and ecstasy we pass;
Wind, sun, and earth remain, the birds sing still,
When we are old, are old . . .' 'And when we die
  All's over that is ours; and life burns on
Through other lovers, other lips,' said I,
  'Heart of my heart, our heaven is now, is won!'

'We are Earth's best, that learnt her lesson here.
  Life is our cry. We have kept the faith!' we said;
  'We shall go down with unreluctant tread
Rose-crowned into the darkness!' . . . Proud we were,
And laughed, that had such brave true things to say.
–And then you suddenly cried, and turned away.